THE *little* BOOK OF

TURNING

40

books by
BOXER

www.booksbyboxer.com

Published in the UK by
Books By Boxer, Leeds, LS13 4BS
© Books By Boxer 2016
All Rights Reserved

ISBN: 9781909732001

The end of life
begins at 40.

40

40

When you turn 40,
forgetfulness is
more believable.

The lovely thing about being forty is that you can appreciate 25-year-old men.

(Colleen McCullough)

When you turn 40,
you start to prefer the
sofa to the nightclub.

Remember...
even David Beckham
is over 40.

Life begins at 40.

(W. B. Pitkin)

40

Once we hit forty,
women only have about
four taste buds left:
one for vodka, one for
wine, one for cheese
and one for chocolate.

(Gina Barreca)

40 = closer to free travel/bus pass.

Advice for turning 40:
Install more mirrors
to spot grey hairs
or baldness.

Advice for turning 40:
Buy a bigger cake...
It will look like
there are less candles!

Wrinkles are just signs
of a happy past.

The word old gets
older with age.

40   40

When you reach 40,
you know who your
true friends are...
Since they've stuck
around for so long!

The older you are,
the fewer mistakes
you can make.

40 = closer to
pensioner discounts.

40 ☆ ☆ ☆ **40**

☆

☆

Old enough to know
right from wrong and
young enough to make
the wrong choice!

The older you get,
the easier it is to get
a seat on the bus.

40

40

40...
It's just a number.
(A damn big one!)

If life begins at 40, you know you've been dead for 39 years.

(John Lennon)

Old enough to give
advice, young enough
not to take it.

40 40

40

Oh to be only half as wonderful as my child thought I was when he was small, and only half as stupid as my teenager now thinks I am.

(Rebecca Richards)

Forty is the age when you stop patting yourself on the head and start under the chin.

You know you've
reached middle
age when your
weightlifting consists
merely of standing up.

(Bob Hope)

40

40

40

When women pass thirty, they forget their age. When forty, forget they ever remembered it.

(Ninon de Lenclos)

39 is a nice age for a woman, especially if she happens to be 47.

She claims she just turned 30. It must have been a U turn!

You know you're getting old when everything hurts. And what doesn't hurt doesn't work.

(Hy Gardner)

40

40

The older I get, the better I used to be.

(John McEnroe)

40

40

I'm now at the age where I've got to prove that I'm just as good as I never was.

(Rex Harrison)

40

40

40 **40**

At the age of 20 we don't care what the world thinks of us. At 30 we worry deeply about what it thinks of us. At 40 we realise it isn't thinking of us at all.

(Herbert Prochnow)

40

Children despise their
parents until the age
of 40, when they
suddenly become
just like them, thus
preserving the pattern.

(Quentin Crewe)

There's only one cure for grey hair. The French invented it. It's called the guillotine.

40

40

40

40

After 40 a woman has to choose between losing her face or her figure. My advice is to keep your face and stay sitting down.

(Barbara Cartland)

40 **40**

An archeologist is
the best husband any
woman can have. The
older she gets, the more
interested he is in her.

(Agatha Christie)

She finally admitted
she was 40 – she just
didn't say when.

It's just as well to be
told you're too old nt 40;
then you're over it.

(Grace Murney Hooper)

One of the hardest
decisions in life is
wondering when to
start middle age.

(Clive James)

At 40 a woman
is just about old
enough to start
looking younger.

(Katharine Whitehorn)

Age is a question of mind over matter. If you don't mind, it doesn't matter.

(Dan Ingman)

40 40

I'm at the age where
my back goes out
more than I do.

(Phyllis Diller)

40

When I was 40 my doctor
advised me that a man in his
forties shouldn't play tennis.
I heeded his advice carefully
and could hardly wait until I
reached 50 to start again.

(Hugo Black)

A woman past 40
should make up her
mind to be young,
not her face.

(Billie Burke)

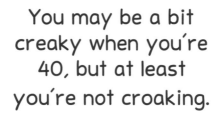

You may be a bit creaky when you're 40, but at least you're not croaking.

(Melanie White)

40

40

40 is the new 30
that feels like 50.

You know you're getting older when you try to straighten out the wrinkles in your socks and discover you're not wearing any.

(Leonard Knott)

Middle age is when you're sitting at home on a Saturday night and the phone rings and you hope it's not for you.

(Ogden Nash)

Middle age is that time in a man's life when his daydreams centre around a bank manager saying yes instead of a girl.

(Jane Fonda)

There are three signs of old age: you forget names, you forget faces and...

(Red Skelton)

40 = knowing you are getting closer to that retirement fund.

40 is your chance to get a tattoo before it's like drawing on a deflated balloon.

40

Turning 40 still doesn't mean it is socially acceptable to join a book club.

40 is the old age
of youth.
(But 50 is the
youth of old age)

Smile when you
are 40 -
it's harder to
dribble from an
upturned mouth.

40

40 is a good age
to put on weight -
it'll stretch out
your wrinkles.

40

Being 40 makes
you better in bed*

(*Just at sleeping!)

Forty – the new
F word. Fabulous!

(Unknown)

40

40

You know you've reached forty when your little black book doesn't have the numbers of old flames in it anymore, but GPs.

Most women aren't as young as they're painted.

(Max Beerbohm)

On my 40th birthday
my son gave me a card
saying 'Life begins at 40.'
Underneath, written in
smaller letters, was
'But so does rheumatism,
arthritis, lumbago,
sciatica, constipation
and myopia.'

(Anon)

I'm not like Jane Fonda or any of those other women who say how fabulous they think it is to turn forty. The truth is, it's a crock of shit.

(Cher)

When a man of 40 falls in love with a girl of 20, it's not her youth he's seeking, but his own.

(Lenore Coffee)

40 40 40 40

I believe in loyalty.
When a woman reaches
an age she likes, she
should stick to it.

(Eva Gabor)

This actress I knew, when I was 31, she was 36. When I got to 40, she was 37. That must have been some year!

(Tony Curtis)

40

40

At 16 I was stupid, insecure and indecisive. At 25 I was wise, self-confident, prepossessing and assertive. At 45 I am stupid, confused, insecure and indecisive. Who would have supposed that maturity is only a short break in adolescence?

(Jules Pfeiffer)

40

One of the many things nobody ever tells you about middle age, is that it's such a nice change from being young.

(Dorothy Canfield Fisher)

If you are about to go 'over the hill', stop worrying about it. Get over it!

40, mature like a fine old cheese. (Crusty, crumbly, blue-veined and strong smelling!)

The secret to staying young is live honestly, eat slowly and lie about your age.

(Lucille Ball)

40
40
40

A woman is as
young as her knees.

(Mary Quant)

This wine is forty years old. It certainly doesn't show its age.

(Cicero)

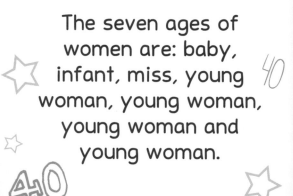

The seven ages of women are: baby, infant, miss, young woman, young woman, young woman and young woman.

When Marlene Dietrich complained to her photographer that he wasn't making her look as beautiful as he used to, he told her, 'I'm sorry Marlene, but I'm seven years older now.'

40
40
40

An actress once said to Rosalind Russell, 'I dread the thought of 45.' Russell looked at her and asked, 'Why, what happened?'

40

40

She's been
pressing forty so
long, it's pleated.

A doctor told me jogging would add ten years to my life. I told him, 'Yeah, since I began I feel ten years older!'

(Lee Travino)

As long as you can
still be disappointed,
you're still young.

(Sarah Churchill)

You know you're getting old when your idea of a hot flaming desire is a barbecued steak.

(Victoria Fabiano)

A very old 12.

(Noel Coward when asked
how a female acquaintance
looked after a face lift.)

Women over 40 are
at their best, but men
over 30 are too old
to recognise it.

(Jean Paul Belmondo)

I am just turning 40, and taking my time about it.

(Harold Lloyd at 77 after being asked his age by a journalist from The Times.)

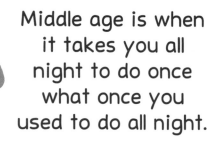

Middle age is when it takes you all night to do once what once you used to do all night.

(Kenny Everett)

'Preparing for the worst' is an activity I have taken up since I turned 35 and the worst actually began to happen just then.

(Delia Ephron)

40

You know you've reached middle age when you toss up between two alternatives and plump for the one that gets you home by nine o'clock.

(Ronald Reagan)

Pushing forty?
On the contrary,
she's clinging onto
it for dear life!

(Ivy Compton-Burnett of
an acquaintance.)

Middle age is when
work is a lot less
fun, and fun is a
lot more work.

(Milton Berle)

40

40

40 is the first time
you realise you can't
do it the second time.
50 is the second time
you realise you can't
do it the first time.

(Mort Sahl)

The great comfort
of turning 40 is
the realisation that
you are now too
old to die young.

(Paul Dickson)

The best years of
Joan Collins' life
were the ten years
between 39 and 40.

Every man over 40
is a scoundrel.

(George Bernard Shaw)

Zsa Zsa Gabor has just celebrated the 41st anniversary of her 39th birthday.

(Joan Rivers)

My age is 39 plus tax.

(Liberace)

40